The Forest at Dawn

by Lorraine Sintetos
illustrations by Kate Flanagan

Harcourt Brace & Company

Orlando Atlanta Austin Boston San Francisco Chicago Dallas New York Toronto London

It's almost dawn. White snow lies on the mountaintops.

Autumn and winter have already passed. The river has thawed. Animals begin to crawl through the forest.

All the forest animals come to the water. A tawny fawn drinks.

The fawn stops. He finds grass to eat beside the water. The fawn's jaws work slowly.

The fawn looks around, always alert. His mother has taught him the forest law—always watch! Don't get caught!

He hears a cough. The fawn stops walking. What caused that noise? The fawn pauses.

Caw! Caw! A squad of crows squawks. Then a hawk cries. "Be quiet!" she seems to say. The birds stop squawking.

Now the tawny fawn
does not need to run into the
forest. He walks to the water.
He licks a rock.

Who bawls in that straw nest? Tiny, scrawny hawks cry. Why? Because Mother hasn't brought food for a while.

Mother Hawk sees something crawling in the grass. She's caught it! The baby hawks will have their breakfast.

A chipmunk claws at a nut with his paws. He sits and gnaws on the nut with strong jaws.

The chipmunk digs with his claws. He hauled nuts here last fall and knows there ought to be more.

A snake crawls over a rock. She sprawls in the sun and yawns. Will the chipmunk be caught?

The chipmunk sees her and runs away. He, too, knows the forest law—always watch! Don't get caught!

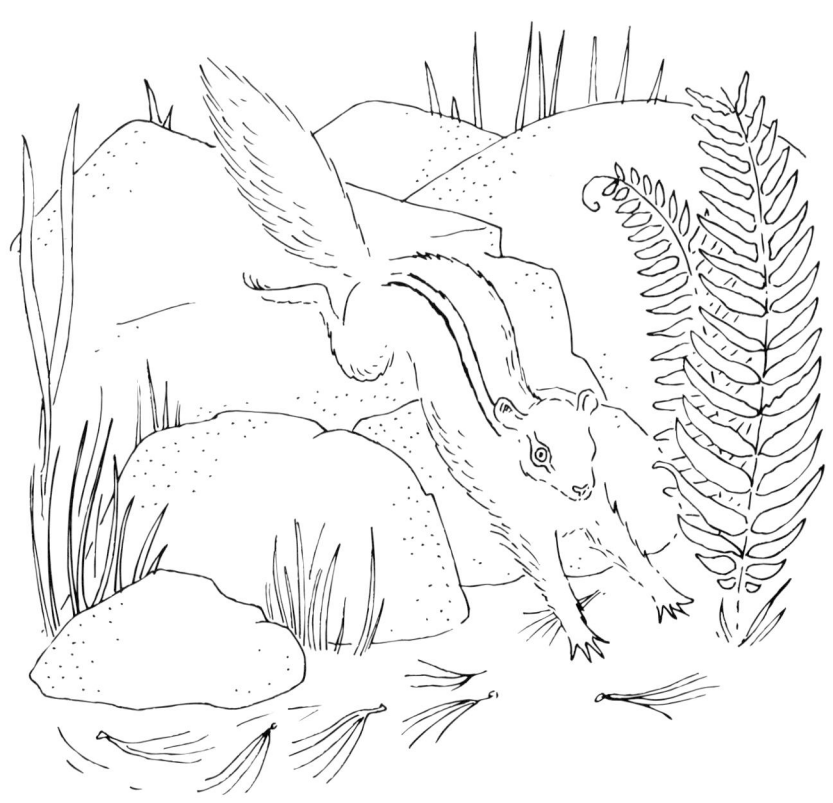

Have you walked in the forest at dawn? Did you see animals, large and small? Did the animals see you?